Mentoring Startup Entrepreneurs Part IV

Business Ideas and Entrepreneurship

Dhananjaya Parkhe

1st Edition

Chapter Name 1
Mentoring Startup Entrepreneurs Part IV
Do we have "Initiative"?
First Thing First

5

Chapter Name 2
Think like a Startup Entrepreneur
Needs a Mindset

8

Chapter Name 3
Types of Startups in India
Broad Categories

11

Chapter Name 4
First Timer- StartPreneur
Difficulties

13

Chapter Name 5
Validating a Business Idea
Startpreneurs Personal Filters

15

Chapter Name 6
True Story.
Honesty and Integrity= Longevity and Sustainability Longevity and Sustainability

18

Chapter Name 7
Zero Defect, Zero Effect, Make in India
And Jevon's Paradox

20

Chapter Name 8　　　　　　　　　　　　　　　　　　　　24
Hofstadter's Law
It always takes longer than you expect.

Chapter Name 9　　　　　　　　　　　　　　　　　　　　25
So? You are looking for a VC?
KNOW what a VC is looking for?

Chapter Name 10　　　　　　　　　　　　　　　　　　　26
Startpreneur/Entrepreneur Mindset
Concluding Part IV

Mentoring Startup Entrepreneurs Part IV

In the previous three parts, we discussed about Mentoring, Choice of Right Mentor, Different Compliance requirements and my personal experiences in Mentoring Startup and Entrepreneurs. In this Part, we shall discuss things specific to Entrepreneurs.

The first step for an entrepreneur before starting a new business is finding right idea for their startup. By thinking up a good start up idea is not the right way per me. ideal way is to watch for problems and needs around us, preferably problems and needs that we have faced our self. Or what we have seen other people, our friends or family, face regularly.

I always say, "Just by watching we can observe a lot. We need to be very observant. Why should we work on such problems? Firstly, we ensure that the problem exists and the First step is to work on problems that exist, needs that exist. One common cause of failure is to try and startups trying to solve problems no one faces, needs that do not exist.

Getting Started

The aim should be to solve a problem that exists. By observing we shall know that we can look for pain points that individuals or businesses face, that can help us arrive at our venture idea whether for a Product or a Service or a Convergence of two in a Productized Service depending upon the personal strengths of the Startup Entrepreneurs.

.

Chapter Number 1
Do we have "Finishiative"?
First Thing First

Years ago, I said to my Mentees that "Initiative is not enough, we need to have Finishiative too!" For a Startup Entrepreneurs' mindset, this is very critical. If we can stay focused on our Goal and "Keep at It" till we reach the Finish Line and achieve the Goal is a critical attribute/ quality required in any Entrepreneur.
If we recall the old saying" Never put off until tomorrow what we can do today" tells us about setting our Priorities and when it comes to starting our own business, this saying hits the nail right on the head.

Our business is only going to come to life if we do the things we need to do to bring it to fruition. If we continue to put off the things we need to do to get our business started until tomorrow--we're too busy at work, or our kids need we to pick them up at the mall, our spouse wants we to watch a popular new television show--then when will we ever get around to doing them?

Starting a successful business takes more than thinking about it, talking about it, or dreaming about it. It takes more than telling our friends that we would like to start our own business someday. It takes more than reading a copy of a magazine or two. It takes more than reading this eBook.

Starting a business requires action--we need to set goals, establish tasks, and then complete them. It's not the size of the goals or the tasks that counts, it's the doing that is everything. Fnishiative gives the best satisfaction – it is my humble personal experience.

The number-one ingredient for success in of Startup is "starting" and growing a business is something all of us do in varying quantities: Finishiative is what some would call as the "Completion of Finish Line Gene or what I choose to call as **Finishiative Gene**" which is present in all of us and just needs the right Mentor spark to ignite it.

The Finishiative Gene is habit based on psychological need to follow through on what we start and take it to its logical end--whether it is preparation of a proposal, working on a project for a client, or seeing a business through its rhythmic/ non-rhythmic cycles including turbulent times and up/down cycles. In short, the Finishiative Gene is what separates successful MSME Entrepreneurs from the wannabe Startups, and it can have the biggest positive impact on our success as an entrepreneur.

So, what are the key molecules of this Finishiative Gene? There are two as in a typical Gene:
1. The promoter (with or without an Incubator or Accelerator) is the part of the **gene** that determines when and where it will be expressed.
2. The coding region is the part of the **gene** that dictates the sequence of the (protein etc.) encoded by the **gene**.

1. The promoter Goal in the Short term: **Get things done**. This is Setting a daily routine, Daily Action plan like wake up every morning and take right number of steps towards achieving our goals. Each day would be filled with small number of activities like buying business cars, applying for registration of business, hiring a lawyer, hiring a chartered Accountant to help we incorporate business etc. Or it may mean doing desk research on the internet, doing tele-survey calls to prospects to find out about their needs/ problems and whether the Product/ Service/ Productized Service we intend to market will be acceptable to them. We can build a business by taking some of these and other important, short-term, but important, steps. In a way, the Promoter here researches, prepares ground, lays plinth in short measurable steps for the long term building of a skyscraper like building.

2. **The coding region** is what I call as Long term: The important attribute and quality required in an Entrepreneur is **Persistence**. Few businesses are known to have tasted overnight success. The latest hot product or Service provider is usually the result of years of hard work and perseverance. My friend is a Doctor's husband and they run a Hospital and a charity. He tells me from experience that a Clinic/ Polyclinic or a small new Hospital has a success ratio of only 5% and 95% or the Doctors / Promoters fail. Reason: They want to be overnight successes which it takes 4-5 years of hard work and perseverance and good word of mouth publicity for them to earn a good name, fame and worthwhile practice. The break-even may happen sooner but Success which is fulfillment of their dream takes longer. We might have the greatest but, if we aren't willing or able to hang in with it for the long haul, then we'll

potentially miss enjoying the gold at the end of our rainbow. I, therefore, term the Coding Region of the business enterprise to be in a PERPETUAL BETA state forever coming out with improved Versions 1.0, 1,1,2.0,3.0 etc. and doing a constant make-over with customer feedback, satisfaction surveys – forever listening to customers and market and making improvements which keeps us ahead of the competition.

We may think we were not born with the Finishiative Gene but, trust me, it resides deep inside us. The Finishiative Gene is present in all of us, it's standard ORIGINAL EQUIPMENT and a God's Gift from HIS factory. If we haven't seen our FINISHIATIVE Gene lately, we might need to dust it off before we'll have an opportunity to give it a workout. The more we exercise it, the stronger it will get. And the stronger it gets, the closer we will be to living our dreams instead of just dreaming them.
I also say this rather loudly to my Mentees "If we can't Dream BIG, STOP Dreaming!". Finishiative Gene, Promoters' spirit and a Coders' Perpetual Beta persistence are keys to making the dreams come true.

Chapter Number 2
Thinking like a Startup Entrepreneur
Needs a Mindset

The Entrepreneur Mindset

What is then, my Entrepreneur or StartPreneur Mindset:

1. We have an eye on the Goal all the time.

We are quick to gauge opportunity from a distance. Successful entrepreneurs have this trait in common - they have a keen eye for finding an opportunity. Their vision as Entrepreneurs/ Startpreneurs is different. We see 'business opportunities' on the horizon. For e.g. people in an upcoming suburb are complaining about not availability of a Hypermart for Groceries or a Supermarket; the entrepreneur sees Profit - an opportunity to open a profitable Corner/convenient store. They have their eyes open and have the courage to grab them.

2. B+Ve– need not be your Blood Group

You may or may not have B+Ve blood group yet you can be Positive and optimistic. Be optimistic. Startpreneurs and Entrepreneurs both need positive outlook. Positive thinking makes open to many options and possibilities and a mentality to experiment with commitment and passion. Optimism coupled with an ability to do Reality checks, hard due diligence on our own helps us to be careful. Careful optimism helps us be aware of the possible risks and helps us to plan mitigation of risks in our minds. My usual advice to my Mentees is to do a PESTLE Analysis quickly whenever they have found an opportunity. It need not be elaborate, power point based – quick check of facts and the available information found thru internet desk research can be helpful.

3. No pessimism – Only Tough-minded Optimism

Pessimism vs Tough Minded Optimism. In business, Pessimism may help assume potential problems and Risks. While some degree of pessimism may be good, it can bog you down. If used to 'identification of problems' it may be useful. I recommend Tough-Minded Optimism which not just identifies, acknowledges- it makes us go into our reserves of courage and optimism with a Tough Mind – the mind which is ready to resolve problems – after all, when we solve others' problems then only we see opportunities of making Profit.

4. Long-Term Vision.

A person with a normal vision is said to be 6/6 or 20/20 Vision. The entrepreneurs have "Vision", which is a developed 'Sense' and a much-developed faculty to foresee – display foresight and almost an intuitive predictive ability about Long-Term Vision. The Long-term Vision that sees success of the future today. They think ahead and imagine in their mind what the following days and years have in store. The entrepreneurs make it a practice to watch current news, trends, patterns of changes. I always say this to my Mentees "Just by keenly Watching- You Can Observe a Lot". This helps in shaping the Long-Term Vison. This helps entrepreneurs know what to anticipate, how to take advantage of the situations for benefit/ Profit. My friend watched the trend of commodities/ precious commodities and stored Silver as per his capacity and sold at a huge profit later. "Profit", Dr. S.L. Kirloskar is believed to have said "is not a bad word". The attribution of Excessive Profit/ Profiteering is bad as per law too. But More about PROFIT subject some other time.

5. Profit happens when you make it in Purchase and in Sales.
I learnt it as a translation of a Lakshmi Mantra on Lakshmi Puja day in Indian Festival of lights Diwali. It says "Lakshmi Maiya Teri Krupa Ho, Kray Mein Bhi Fayda Ho aur Vikray me bhi Fayda ho!". Translates as "O, Goddess Lakshmi (Goddess of business and Prosperity and wealth) make me able to make profit in all I purchase and all that I Sell". The Startpreneur/ Entrepreneur takes steps after due thought. It is called prudence.

None of the successful Mentees I have Mentored ever jumped into businesses recklessly or just to follow a bandwagon. Whim is not fancy here. My advice is to spend time in research, brainstorming when you have a partner or two or with your mentor, incubator, accelerator. Research, including desk research, study and thinking things through is my honest recommendation to my Mentees. One of my network connections specializes in Cost reduction, Cost savings thru Purchase management and has even developed elaborate system to teach entrepreneurs about the system. It is a profitable business for him and the learners of the system. A Win Win. Making Profit thru good Pricing decisions with a Sales Process is the usual way of making profit. One of the largest business houses Purchase VP once told me "In our organization we squeeze the suppliers to give us the best price and credit / delivery terms without compromising the Quality".

His KPI in business is how much competitiveness he and his team improved which helped the company and their contribution is well rewarded. The company recently is disrupting a mass consumer market with its Product, Service and a combination of disruptive Productized Service. There is no shame in making Profit. This company has a great record of Dividends and Bonus shares and the belief is that their "Customers and Shareholders must make money all the time".

Chapter Number 3
Types of Start-ups in India
Broad Categories

We give below a very broad categorization of Start-ups in India for the Startpreneur/ Entrepreneur reading this.

MSMEs – The Nodal Ministry is called Micro, Small, Medium Enterprises Ministry and there is perhaps a linkage with the MSDE or the Ministry for Skills Development and Entrepreneurship although, I am a bit skeptical of the roles they respectively play in helping and developing the Entrepreneurship in India. For Mentoring, there are fancy Association websites which may be put into morgue due to inactivity. The is not very conducive although a senior government official claimed that over 1200 hurdles (!) in the way of the Entrepreneurs have been removed. While I support the Government but I am not a blind follower and the reality I see is rather bleak when it comes to Startup India Registration onward to taking loans from Mudra Bank etc. It is clearly not an easy path for entrepreneurs in India. .

1. Category of the Startups are all companies which that have a potential to scale, are looking at transforming unorganized sector and a large market with the use of minimum technology. They are recognized by their limited vision, non-availability of guidance, mentoring, they use commoditized technology to run their services businesses in the areas which they have identified as 'Need' areas to solve problems of a limited geography/ demography. Their dependence on offline operators is high.

For E.g. Meru-Cabs, Fast=track, Tab-Cab, KSTDC, Airport Taxi (the technology usage being, mobile/ phone lines, instead of someone having to walk up to an auto or cab/ taxi-stand and hail a cab) to give an example from the Local Taxi / travel business operated by an individual.

2. Technology Startup in similar space would be –a company which leverages technology efficiently to achieve scale and improve the experience of the end-user or customer experience, provides new features, competitive advantages and new ways of doing business.

E.g. Uber / Ola (the tech being smart phones, GPS maps, Music, Free WiFi, Video on

Demand etc and Digital payment using wallets, credit cards apart from Cash and offering credit), Amazon, Snapdeal, Shopclues, PaytmMall, Flipkart etc. There is still a component of offline operations with these companies, which are crucial, but not as intense as "startups".

3. Hi-technology startups - Companies which are in the business of building self-driven cars, electric scooters, or the metro trains of the future generation, or advanced robotics or Artificial Intelligence. These companies provide building blocks for technology startups to achieve scale and efficiency. They own technology patents and help achieve technology independence.

Chapter Number 4
First Timer - StartPreneur
Difficulties

First time entrepreneurs often get confused because they get such conflicting advice. They talk to five different people who they tell them ten different things, which is why founders are never sure whether they are on the right track.

Many mentor's advice that you should be passionate - that you should dream big and follow your dreams because your goal should be to change the world. They tell us to emulate heroes like Steve Jobs and Elon Musk who could implement their dreams and create companies which have changed the way we live our lives. Yes, this is the holy grail, and it's well worth aiming for! We all want our children to be ambitious because there is so much which they can accomplish, and we want them to make the most of their potential. Having said this, we also tell founders to not bite off more than you can chew. Yes, it's important that a man's reach should exceed his grasp, but you do need to remember that you have real-world constraints, and you should be aware of these. We don't want to clip your wings, but you must battle well-funded competitors with deep pockets; other startups are happy to steal your lunch; raising money is always an ongoing battle; delighting fickle customers is always a challenge; and there are the unknown unknowns to trip you up. It's hard to attract A players, and keeping morale high when you are not sure how you will be able to pay next month's salaries can drive you nuts.

The risk is that if you try to do too much all at the same time, you'll end up accomplishing nothing at all. You'll burn through money quickly, and your dreams will get converted to nightmares because you are over-stretched. Therefore, it's so important to learn what not to do. It's essential that you learn to focus, and knowing how and what to prioritize is a key skill every founder needs to master.

So is the founder meant to create business plans which show how she will achieve world domination? Or should she show how she can quickly achieve profitability? Either way, there will be criticism. One group will say she's not able to think big; while others will mock her for trying to aim for the moon. It's because of these mixed messages that entrepreneurs get completely confused.

The trick is to find the right balance. We don't have to be pessimistic, and we don't want you to be over-optimistic either and find that you have run out of steam even before completing the first lap. Remember that you are running a marathon, and you don't want to run out of money, steam and stamina! You need to look for the golden mean, where you can show that you have a sensible approach which balances short term pain with long term gains. Yes, this is hard to do, but no one said being an entrepreneur would be easy.

The key is that you should have a well-defined plan, and the courage of your convictions to stick to it, no matter what anyone else says and does. Learning how to meditate can help you find your true North Star and keep your balance!

Chapter Number 5
Validate a Business Idea (How?)
Sharpeners Personal Personal Filters

You write a book but you don't get a Reader. You are a Model/ budding Star and post your picture on Social Media but do not get a single Like. It is said that Coke sole only some 2 Dozen bottles in the first year. The harsh truth is, we may spend years in perfecting the building, but when we launch, our product may still not get any buyers. Nary a startup work hard for months/ years on perfecting their idea and get dejected/ demotivated that they did not score well in the market place. The Solution they painfully found for people has no takers.

What therefore, the Startpreneurs and Entrepreneurs launching new products, services or productized services should do is create their own Idea Assessment filters to realistically estimate the time to market and the time of actual acceptance. Marketing costs factoring will then be more realistic. The success and failure can be pre=determined by asking some tough questions. These questions assist Startpreneurs get a firsthand validation about their idea.

1. Which problem are you trying to solve by launch of your product/ service / productized service. If we are unable to respond to this question we may not have a successful idea.
2. Have others people attempted to solve same problem before, and do you know why did their solutions/ product/ service/ productized service succeed or fail? did. While starting my first Courier / consolidator business I visited over 200 courier shops and asked overt/ covert questions (as decoy customer) to find out what kept them in the business/ what makes them tick, what made growth possible.
3. How many specific benefits for your product or idea can you list? The more you can think of, the more likely it is that you're meeting a real need and can be successful.
4. Can you state, in clear language, the key features of your product or service? Not being able to easily describe the key features of your idea is a warning sign that the idea isn't well thought out yet
5. Does your idea already exist in the same way you were going to create it? If a similar solution exists, how will yours be different? If you don't have any clear differentiating benefits or features, you likely need a new idea
6. Who are your potential competitors?

Having competitors isn't a bad thing -- it means a market exists. However, knowing what you'll face if you launch is important, as an overcrowded marketplace or one where consumers have a strong affinity for the dominant brand may be more difficult to break into.

7. What key features does my product or service have that others will have a hard time copying? Before you go into business, you need to be very clear about what sets you apart from competitors.
8. Have you done a SWOT analysis? This framework helps you to understand the strengths, weaknesses, opportunities and threats that your idea has, giving you a better idea of the overall likelihood for success.
9. Do you have access to the various resources you need to launch a business? While you don't need to be rich to launch a business, you will need some combination of time and money, depending on the scope of your idea. If you have no way to access everything you need, you're better off waiting to launch your company until your situation is different.
10. Do you have a mentor or industry advisor that you can call on? Certainly, you can do it alone if you have to, but when you start a new business, having the advice of others in a similar business space can prevent unnecessary expenditures or missteps.
11. Can you name somebody who would benefit from your product or service? This is the beginning of market research -- who do you actually know that would use your idea? A general demographic isn't enough, so take the time to hone in your target buyer personas.
12. What is the size of the market that will buy your product or service? If you don't know the size of the market, you have a lot of research ahead of you. Understanding how many people need your idea -- and what they're willing to pay for it -- will help you determine whether your concept is viable.
13. Have you reached out to potential customers for feedback? Getting feedback before investing further money can help you avoid creating a product or service that nobody really wants.
14. Can you set up a landing page and encourage interested people to sign up for more information. This can be an easy and inexpensive way to test interest in a product or service. If a lot of people are interested, it's a great sign that you're on the right track!
15. What would it take to build a minimum viable product to test the market? One mistake many entrepreneurs make is thinking that they must launch a finished concept right away. Consider starting small, gauging interest and iterating as you go.
16. Can you get paying customers from your target market to pre-order based on a

blueprint or mockup? Pre-orders are a solid sign of customer commitment. Someone saying they're interested is one thing, but seeing people actually pony up their credit card information is a much stronger sign of potential success.

17. Can you produce the actual product yourself, or do you have a partner who can? As you might expect, before launch, you need to know who's actually going to produce the first set of products or services, as well as whether they can do so within your budget.
18. Do you have distributors or partners to help you scale your business? Once you have paying customers, you'll need to ramp up actual distribution to meet demand. Do you have access to the partners and/or money needed to do so?
19. What will it take to break even or make a profit? Some ideas take a lot of upfront investment, while others don't. If yours does, it's a good idea to plan for how you'll handle your finances and daily needs while you're waiting for your product or service to gain traction.
20. How can investors in your idea make a profit? If you want others to come alongside your business and help you grow, you'll have to know how they can benefit.

It may take some time to come up with answers to all these questions, but once you have them, you should have a better idea about how viable your idea is. If it passes these tests, go for it! If not, keep thinking -- may be your next idea will be the one that changes the world.

Chapter Number 6
True Story.

Honesty = Longevity = Sustainability in Business.

Let me share with you today a True Story.

Ever since I Retired and began my morning Walks I also developed a liking to the Morning Cuppa Kapi (South Indian foaming Coffee in a glass for the uninitiated) and found 2-3 different Kerb Kapi shops who served me Less Sugar Coffee I.e. Coffee with NO SUGAR!

They serve it in the glass, Steel cup or in a disposable coffee cup. These are truly economy class but great Taste stuff made of Ground Seed Coffee decoction mixed with boiling water/ water mixed Milk in a steaming cup semi-filled with the Foam. It is truly habit forming and I like to indulge in this although I change the kerb shops every now and then depending upon the urge to take a short stop on my long walks and catch my breath.

This story is about a small enterprising family consisting of a Husband and wife who ran the corner/ kerb store mainly serving Tea/ Coffee on the ground floor shop while they lived on the 1st floor. Wife made tea/ coffee in an ante room and filled in special thermos with a dispenser which is available to my knowledge only in Southern India. The husband would attend to customers – take orders serve tea, coffee, cigarette, gutka, raw tobacco, sweets, snacks and occasionally heat up the veg/ non-veg puffs etc. As they opened shop at sharp 6.30 AM they had customers right early in the morning and probably they closed shop well after 11 PM when the hotel opposite would close.

The shortage of coins in India is a well-known one and most shopkeepers use the opportunity for profit by giving chocolates in place of coins change and make 100% profit. Our man in the story was different. He knew I am a diabetic and drink Less Sugar Coffee and he would keep count of the change due to me rather than giving me chocolates. At the end of the week or so, he would tell me not to pay as he was adjusting the change money accumulated by him. I felt so happy about his honesty as he has over 1000 footfalls a day and to remember my short change of Rs. 1 or 2 for 5-6 consecutive days and give me the adjustment Coffee was a great act of honesty. This went on for past couple of years.

Last three months though, things appeared different with him. He did not return the change or give me adjustment coffee even once and I thought may be, he has increased the Coffee rates.

This month, suddenly I saw 2-3 different people manning the shop. They are quite efficient and fast and have seemingly understood every client's requirements and serve all regular customers without asking 'What do you want'. The shop is very well stocked all the time and the refill service from different vendors is queueing up and it appears their business is booming. They also returned my due change for the Coffee promptly every single day.

It made me wonder what happened. I thought the guy and his wife have gone for holidays and his relatives are manning the shop. Then I came to know – he was running debt and had to sell off the room and the shop to the lenders who put people in the same business to run the show as the customers was used to coming for Tea, coffee or other items to this place without fail.

It reminds me of a friend of mine who was into small lending at high interest rates but with no security to small businesses. Once I saw him funding a Barber shop for the Chair and security deposit for the shop and his logic was simple. Small businessmen rarely fail on repayment and rarely default. Having worked in village branch of a bank I agree with him – it is true.

In this case, though, it appeared to be false. Not only I saw a Merger/ Acquisition of a small business by the lender but infusion of new capital and new trained manpower to grow the business by ousting the current owner.

Which brings me to the important learnings I have had in my life about businesses. I often repeat this 'If the foundation of the business is laid on falsehood, dishonesty and unethical practices – the business is certain to go but – the doom is easily predicted'.

The tell-tale signs of not returning the small change – when he was in the habit to return it earlier must talk about the agony, pain the earlier owner of the shop must have undergone to make this habit change. But this habit also reflected on his character and the continuance led to his doom probably much earlier than many big businesses which manage to survive this for longer durations.

However, I always feel for the Small businesses and feel sorry if they make losses or small entrepreneurs must go out of business due to loan sharks ever present in every town of India.

Long ago, in a Palmistry book I had read – "Character is Fixed, The Personality Develops."

My understanding was Character is unchanged even if the person is under extreme stress but when I see incidents like these I feel Character is 'Fixed' like a Fixed cricket match – a make believe and one wonders whom to trust?

Chapter Number 7
Zero Defect, Zero Effect, Make in India
and Jevon's Paradox.

Prime Minister Narendra Modi of India recently announced on 68th Independence Day :

1. Manufacturers of World are invited to come to India and **'Make in India'** as India has the Talent pool, Resources and facilities.

2. Asked for a Focus on Quality and **Zero Defect** while maintaining Zero Environmental impact or **Zero Effect** as he called it.

Great thinking. Great Slogans for a Resurgent India aiming to improve its falling GDP Growth rate of past couple of years and bounce back on the back of the strength of its New Government and Primarily on the strength of the Manufacturing Sector.

3. The Third and moot point (he made) of course was to boost the Indian Pride by promoting **'Made in India'** as a Brand.

This reminded me of a Paradox I had read some time ago called " Jevon's Paradox".

No. The Business Schools (at least where I have taught) do not teach this. May be, the Schools of Economics still do.

Let us first examine how **Wikipedia** describes <u>Jevon's Paradox:</u>

This Paradox seems to have originated from Coal-burning factories in the 19th Century Manchester, England.

- <u>Improved technology allowed coal to fuel the Industrial Revolution</u>
- <u>Thereby greatly increasing the consumption of coal.</u>

In economics, the **Jevons paradox** (sometimes **Jevons effect**) <u>is the proposition</u> that: as technology progresses, the increase in efficiency with which a resource is used tends to increase (rather than decrease) the rate of consumption of that resource.

- In 1865, the English economist William Stanley Jevons observed that technological

- improvements that increased the efficiency of coal-use led to the increased consumption of coal in a wide range of industries.

- He argued that, contrary to common intuition, technological improvements could not be relied upon to reduce fuel consumption.

- The issue has been re-examined by modern economists studying consumption rebound effects from improved energy efficiency.

- In addition to reducing the amount needed for a given use, improved efficiency lowers the relative cost of using a resource, which tends to increase the quantity of the resource demanded, potentially counteracting any savings from increased efficiency. Additionally, increased efficiency accelerates economic growth, further increasing the demand for resources.

- The Jevons paradox occurs when the effect from increased demand predominates, causing resource use to increase.

The Jevons paradox has been used to argue that **energy conservation may be futile**, as **increased efficiency may increase fuel use.**

1. Nevertheless, increased efficiency can improve material living standards.

2. Further, fuel use declines if increased efficiency is coupled with a Green Tax or other conservation policies that keep the cost of use the same (or higher).

3. As the Jevons paradox applies only to *technological improvements* that increase fuel efficiency, policies that impose conservation standards and increase costs do not display the paradox.

Few more announcements by the Government of India relating to the Labor laws are equally important.

1. Changes in the Apprenticeship Act

2. Changes in the Overtime hours

3. Allowing Women to work in Night shifts etc.

These are indicators of creating a Productivity climate. These are expected to Work in favor of the Manufacturing and Services Sectors.

The danger I see are therefore two-fold.

A. Dilution of the Environmental Laws to facilitate faster, online clearances may make the

ISO to perhaps re-write the ISO 14001 the Environmental Standard for India. This can certainly raise eye-brows and may become a restrictive issue when it comes to Foreign Trade of Indian Goods.

B. The Work-life Balance may be adversely impacted. While the workers may tend to work more, it can adversely impact the health. Organizations like Social Accountability International and ISO with SA 8000 certified organizations may up their ante' against these as this goes against the grain of the Standards. Leave alone the UN Global Compact and related dangers to workers - India will never be able to aspire for Certifications/ Accreditations for higher standards like 'Investor in People'.

The Growth will happen, no doubt, make in India will happen and the Jevon's Paradox will apply this time on the major Resource - People and that's an Alarm signal to watch out for!

This space will be worth Watching!

Chapter Number 8
Hofstadter's Law
It always takes longer than you expect.

Hofstadter's Law says: "It always takes longer than you expect".

I sincerely feel, Startpreneurs, Entrepreneurs as also all the Medical Practitioners and Surgeons should learn to use this law. As a Cardiac patient asked his Doctor - " How much longer, will I live?"

A very difficult question to answer and extremely full of sensitivities. This Law equips them and gives solace to the Questioner.

Let me share with you the reason why?

I am sure, every car owner and Driver has seen the Side Rear-view Mirrors. The variants quoted here are from the Google Search - they are not part of the OEMs :).

These quotes made me wonder when I was learning to drive. Some of them I found interesting than the standard ones. Judging Distance was a Test we used to have as National Cadet Corps Cadets while preparing for a Rifle shooting with the Ageing Army Instructors would spend couple of hours on this before we even getting to touch a weapon. I remember the Old Driver who was teaching me to drive when I was 16 (Yes, that was under-age of License in India) and would take me thru every printed/ written word before he put me behind the wheels finally! :)

The writing on the Side Rear-view Mirror always says " Object in mirror are closer than they appear". So how does one correctly judge the distance of an approaching vehicle from the side/ behind us?

How does one predicts the events in future. I would ask the Astrologers and Palmists and later when at work to the Company Strategists! :) I one day found a Law which states " It always takes longer than you expect, even when you take into Account Hofstadte's Law".

It was written by Douglas Hofstadter who wrote:

- "In the early days of computer chess, people used to estimate that it would be ten years until a computer (or program) was world champion.

- But after ten years had passed, it seemed that the day a computer would become world champion was still more than ten years away".

I learnt that Hofstadter's law is a self- referential time-related adage, coined by Douglas Hofstadter and it got named after him. The Diagram below explained to me (a visual person, who can only understand by graphics, pictures or visualising).

Hofstadter's Law says: "It always takes longer than you expect, even when you take into account Hofstadter's Law." Hofstadter's Law was a part of Douglas Hofstadter's 1979 bookGödel, Escher, Bach: An Eternal Golden Braid.

- He then suggests that this was **"just one more piece of evidence for the rather recursive Hofstadter's Law."**

- **So now we know! :)**

We came across a great English derivative word called as I explained in prior Chapter," Finishiative" and we liked it. This law is a statement regarding the difficulty of accurately estimating the time it will take to complete tasks of substantial complexity. We thought, this law will help us predict accurately when we can finish the task, project, work assigned.

- It is often cited amongst programmers, especially in discussions of techniques to improve productivity, such as The Mythical Man-Month or Extreme programming.

- The recursive nature of the law is reflection of the widely experienced difficulty of estimating complex tasks despite all best efforts, including knowing that the task is complex.

- The law was initially introduced in connection with a discussion of chess-playing computers, where top-level players were continuously beating machines, even though the machines outweighed the players in recursive analysis.

- The intuition was that the players were able to focus on particular positions instead of following every possible line of play to its conclusion.

Chapter Number 9
So? You are looking for a VC?
Know what a VC is looking for?

A lot of Entrepreneurs often ask me what Investors are looking for in a Startup. Most Investors (are either clueless or) wont tell you this straight to you, but this is their mandate internally on what they are looking for:

1. A potential 200Mn $ Exit in 4-5 years
2. Company + team should raise not more than 40 - 50$ mn to achieve that.
3. A 200mn$ Exit means (100mn in ecomm transactions, or 40mn being a SaaS Business - you get an idea of the multiple - revenue is per year)
4. Going after a large enough market so that there is enough pie in it for your company to grow exponentially without having to fight tooth and nail and burn more cash in fighting competition. Ideally the size that you need to grow should be 2-10% of this market size.
5. A strong moat - doesn't have to be 100% defensible, but a great team with strong execution capabilities is a quasi moat too. If you have patents, awesome. If you have proprietory access to something even better.

Now this doesn't apply for angel Investors - they will invest in what they feel *feels* right, but if you want to raise any institutional capital post that, you are going to have to hit these milestones. Almost all the top tier VC funds have this metric internally that they use to guage.

IMHO, this is also a very good definition of what a startup is as well. Big Market, Wide open opportunity, and a team that has sharp, clean and fast execution to capture that market. That's a startup. Everything else is either a small business or a flailing startup (or will be one).

A lot of folks say that being a "startup" is about culture etc. But the technical answer as to what is a "startup" is the model - and execution. My strong advice is not to try propping up your company to look like this so that it passes through (a reason why investors dont talk about this openly), but atleast to understand your model and realize if it doesnt fit the criteria you need to look at alternate ways to raise capital - or even raise one angel round and then grow this with different sources of capital.

Chapter Number 10
Startpreneur/ Entrepreneur - MINDSET
Concluding Part IV

There is only uncertainty in business. Best of entrepreneurs can also fail periodically. Many prestigious businessmen suffer failures. With my Mentor tips you will be able to lower the risks/ probability of failure – Well, Hopefully! Even If you apply all the tips you learn in this eBook, you may still not be able to see all the problems but may be able to foresee some even before they happen. This can help you take necessary steps to prevent the problem before it occurs and cause unforeseen damage. Of course, all my tips will be difficult to remember. It is advisable that you keep the copy on your Kindle/ Kindle Reader on your Touchpad/ Smartphone and read it again and again whenever you have the time. This is the best way to instill principles in this eBook to your mind.

If this is the first time you're venturing into business, my advice is to start small first. Do not jump into making very large investments. This is because as a Startpreneur you are still learning. And my Series of eBooks may not be enough to teach you everything. I can tell you that experience is still our best teacher. In business, it is THE Truth. We learn in business when we experience things ourselves. The experiential learning is the most valuable for a Startpreneur/ Entrepreneur. Begin small first and learn. Once experienced, you can then aim for higher goals. Don't be in a tearing hurry! Use this eBook Series as a reference. Don't base your decision solely on it. The world of business is governed by many 'unpredictable things'. Learn to act based on the situation. This eBook series is not a solution to the problems that you will face as a businessman. I have designed this eBook series based upon my own and others real experience with you in mind, it is designed to make you a better startpreneur/ entrepreneur someone that can handle problems depending upon the situation.

Good luck with your business venture. Keep dreaming and keep aiming high.

www.ingramcontent.com/pod-product-compliance
Lightning Source LLC
Chambersburg PA
CBHW041307180526
45172CB00003B/1004